How To Find & Keep Great Tenants

Premium Edition

by

Jeffrey Roark

Real Estate Broker, Property Manager, Investor

&

Author of *The Real Estate Property Management Guide*

&

HowToPropertyManage.com

Table of Contents

How To Find & Keep Great Tenants

Top Three Ways to Find Good Vendors

Are You Really Making Money? - Tracking Income & Expenses

Profit & Loss Statements
Five Bookkeeping System Must Haves - Rent Statements,
Balance Sheets, Reports, Budgets

Investment Real Estate Analysis: A Case Study

It's All About Marketing!

If real estate is all about "Location, location, location", then finding & keeping tenants and managing the rental house to maximize its value is all about Marketing.

Over 25 years ago I received my real estate license, and from day one I was amazed at the number of businesses that feed off of the real estate broker!

Admittedly I've always been a little skeptical of the real estate industry, its associations and numerous designations, and the myriad of services that spring up to provide services to the industry.

Here's a list of some of the items that today's real estate practitioner can purchase to promote a house for rent:

- Virtual Tours
- YouTube Videos
- Digital Magazines
- Pre-paid Commission Services
- Refrigerator Magnets
- Brochure Tubes
- Calendars
- Business Cards, extra large, with 4-color glamor photos
- "Customized" Websites with a monthly subscription fee
- Professional Associations with monthly or annual dues
- Numerous Professional Designations
- Elaborate Property Flyers
- Open House Signs
- Sign Riders

- Directional Signs
- Name Riders
- 1-800 Numbers to call for recorded property information
- Talking Signs
- Smart Phone-friendly signs
- Custom-made Sign Posts
- Real Estate Advertising Magazines, 4-color & glossy
- E-mail Marketing Campaigns
- Proprietary Multiple Listing Services with a recurring access fee

All of these items were taken from the most recent issue of just two real estate trade publications.

These items are visible signs of rental house marketing. They create a good feeling for the real estate practitioner and the rental house owner because it's something that can be seen.

Unfortunately this isn't what gets deals done.

The biggest mistake real estate marketers make is to provide too much up-front information about the house for rent. This happens because they do not have a specific objective for their marketing initiatives.

With advertising and marketing, it's important to closely track the ratio between dollars spent and income received as a direct result of each marketing channel.

Often we'll see real estate practitioners and rental house investors spend a lot of money each month on listing services and get nothing in return!

Sometimes these channels provide good marketing exposure. The problem is, usually this is all that rental house owners will do, and then hope that the phone rings or the email inquiries come in.

So What Does Work? - The #1 Marketing Technique

It's simple and pretty basic. Simply, Answer the phone when Renters call!

This does not mean returning calls left on voice mail. This does not mean screening calls with your caller ID. This does not mean returning text messages left on your cell phone. This does not mean responding to emails. It means:

Answer the phone when Renters call!

If you repeat these six simple words . . .

Answer the phone when Renters call!

Until you've got them memorized, you'll be in the top 5% of professional real estate investors, leasing agents, or managers anywhere and will be able to beat the competition hands down.

If your One and Only Marketing Objective is to get Renters to Call you on the telephone so you can talk to them about your house you have for rent, the question is:

"How do you get them to call?"

Top Five Basic Marketing Tools & Equipment

Here are the Top Five Basic Items to keep in your Marketing Toolbox.

Use these and you'll be more effective than 95% of the competition.

The Top Five Basic Items are:

1. Signs
2. Website
3. Property Flyer
4. On-Line Exposure – either inexpensive or free
5. Basic Property Presentation Script – short, simple and to the point

Let's cover each one in more detail.

#1: Signs

If you already have a house for rent or know what geographic area you'll be buying one in, take some time and drive around the area to make note of the 'for lease' signs that the competition is using.

Successful real estate investors understand that this is a critical marketing step, and they'll make this effort each and every time.

Survey the different types of signs being used and pay attention to:

• Sizes of the signs
• Colors that are common
• Message that is being conveyed
• Overall Appearance of the signage

Which signs caught your eye and impressed you the most, and why?

#2: Website

Most renters that are serious about renting the house you have available will prefer to gather some basic information before they contact you. So even if you have only one house to rent it's a great idea to have a website to provide just enough information to encourage the prospect renter call.

Surf the Internet and take a look at what the competition is doing. Make notes of the websites you like and don't like. Which ones make you want to call for more information, and why?

Building a simple, basic website is quick, easy and inexpensive.

Websites and domain names will run a few dollars a month and will end up being the best marketing investment you've ever made. Many hosting companies provide a large number of free drag-and-drop templates for the design of your website.

In most cases your site can be up and running in less than an hour.

I've had great success with Weebly.com, GoDaddy.com and BlueHost.com for hosting, website design and emails services, and with DomainsInSeconds.com for buying domain names.

Domain names can also be selected and purchased from most hosting services, although you may end up spending a few dollars more per year.

Top Six Items to Have on Your Website

For prospective renters to view or to download:

1. Basic Property Flyer – renters want to know what their new house looks like
2. Property Photos - no more than four - maximum
3. Floor Plan – nice to have, but not mandatory
4. Lease Terms & Conditions – how much and for how long
5. Tenant Rental Application – fees, deposits, income qualifications
6. General Information - about the house, the property and the area

Just remember not to provide too much information and don't feel like you have to reinvent the wheel when putting together your marketing.

You're not an advertising agency – you're an owner that wants to get your house rented fast!

Remember, your website isn't a dating site and you're not trying to 'seal the deal' on-line. All you're trying to do is get the prospective house renters to pre-qualify themselves and to get them to call you.

#3: Property Flyer

A basic, one-page property flyer is an effective marketing tool even if you have only one house to rent.

Design the flyer by creating a template that can be re-used for different rentals. When a new rental becomes available all you'll have to do is switch out the photo and update the description.

Here's an example of a very simple property flyers for a single-family house for rent.

Note the template format being used.

#4: Inexpensive On-Line Exposure

Subscription-based websites such as the Regional Multiple Listing services provide acceptable channels for marketing exposure, but I wouldn't hold my breath and expect your house to get rented as a direct result of listing on these sites.

There is one on-line service that we've found to be the single most effective site available.

Best of all it's either free or very low cost, depending on the market your house is in. It's also a great way to reach out to prospects directly and it's an extremely effective way to get a snap shot on what the competition is doing as well.

Craigslist

For years I'd heard of Craiglist.org but had never used it, and had never actually gone on the site. My impression had always been that it was a great place to go if one was looking for garage sales or personal services.

My company was representing the buyer of a 32 unit apartment building that we'd be doing the leasing and property management for after the sale closed.

I learned that the current owner's broker had also handled the leasing and management and had increased the occupancy rate by 30% in less than a year, during a time when tenants were tough to find.

The woman handling the leasing and marketing of the vacant units was very sharp and when I asked her about her leasing success, she told me that she swore by Craiglist.

I didn't say anything, but I thought to myself, "Craigslist? How can that be? I thought Craiglist was for garage sales?"

By coincidence, that same week I was talking with a friend of mine who had founded and sold several businesses and who was obviously very successful. She mentioned she was selling her BMW on Craigslist.

Again I didn't say anything. But my curiosity was peaked. In less than a week two very smart people had endorsed this on-line service, one for marketing a nice sized apartment building and the other for selling a high-end luxury automobile!

So we began experimenting by marketing properties for lease on Craigslist and were shocked – pleasantly - at the increased volume of inquiries and more importantly the rentals that directly resulted from those inquiries.

We post daily on Craigslist, using the Multiple Marketing Messages technique discussed at the end of this chapter, for all of the rentals we lease and manage. About 75% of the prospective renters that we sign-up come from inquiries initially made from one of our ads on Craigslist.

Pretty amazing results for a free on-line service!

#5: Basic Property Presentation

Now that you know how to get prospects to call you, what do you say then the phone actually rings?

When Prospects Call

Here are The Top Three Goals when you answer a prospect's call:

1. Provide Basic Information to the prospective tenant
2. Qualify the prospective tenant enough to schedule the Next Step
3. Set the hook!

Let's cover each objective in more detail.

Goal #1: Provide Basic Information

Always keep in mind that usually the prospective renter for your house will have seen your name and number from your sign while driving around looking for space.

Remember when you did this when you were surveying the market area of your investment property for competitor's signs?

The prospective renter for your house probably has several names and numbers that he wrote down while driving or recorded in his cell phone, and may not remember exactly which property is yours. If this is the case, don't hold it against him and don't screen him out.

Jog his memory instead.

Put together a 30-second descriptive presentation of your rental house, using the same wording and covering the same points that are on the Property Flyer and the Property Website. Expand a little if you like, but the main idea is to reinforce the messages on the flyer and website.

Your presentation should also answer any basic questions or objections before they come up. For example, which appliances are included, the amount of the application fee, and the length of the rental period.

Don't try to cover everything in your presentation.

The idea is to bait the hook so that - after you qualify the tenant - you can meet face-to-face at the property.

Goal #2: Qualify the Prospect

Qualifying prospective tenants should be very clear-cut.

Cover the applicable items a tenant needs in order to rent your house, including the amount of provable gross income, required security, cleaning or pet deposits, and application fees.

Don't belabor these qualifying items or you'll be perceived as difficult to deal with and run the risk of unintentionally turning good prospects away. Just include them as part of your question and answer period.

Goal #3: The Next Step

You've used your Basic Property Presentation to peak the prospective tenant's interest.

You've Qualified The Prospect and are comfortable that they're a good fit for your property.

Now go ahead and move on to The Next Step by setting the hook!

Your goal is to set up a face-to-face meeting with the prospect at your property.

Setting The Hook

The Top Two Ways to Set the Hook are:

#1: Ask Open-Ended questions like,

"The property sounds like a good match for you. Why don't we set up a time to take a look?"
    Don't ask a closed-ended question that can be answered with a "yes" or "no" such as, "Do you want to look at the property?"

#2: Ask Alternative Choice questions to set up a time.

"Is morning or afternoon better for you?" or "Is Monday or Tuesday better for you?"
    Don't ask a closed ended question like, "Do you want to meet Monday?"

Before moving on, let's cover two often over looked areas of marketing.

Knowing Your Competition

Many beginning investors overlook this step.

They've got their rental house and have good basic marketing material. But they completely forget to look at what the competition is doing, as if they're operating in a vacuum!

Just because a prospective renter is calling for more information doesn't mean your property is her first choice. In today's marketplace tenants always have multiple choices and your property just happens to have made it to her short list.

You've already put together your Basic Marketing Materials - Signs, Flyers, Website, On-line Advertising and Presentation. Next, do your competitive research again to validate you pricing and property positioning.

Always make sure to do in-the-field "reality check" research, using on-line resources only as a guide.

Here are the Top Four "Reality Check" Research Techniques to use:

1. Pretend you're a prospective tenant and make sign calls from other rentals for information
2. Look hard at your rental house and the competition. Figure out the area that your prospective renters are going to be coming from, also known as your trade area
3. Think about who the likely renters for your house will be
4. Compare your house to the competition by putting yourself in the renter's shoes

Remember that renters always have choices and that while your house may be on their list, and maybe their short-list, your rental house will almost never be the only option that a prospective renter has.

From this Competitive Research determine the pros and cons of your property and integrate those into your Basic Marketing Materials and Presentation.

If you have trouble being objective about investment property that you own, have a friend give you his un-biased opinion, ask for feedback from tenant prospects, or interview local brokers or property managers.

Multiple Marketing Messages

At this point you've done a lot!

- Your Competitive Research is done. You know how your competition is positioned, have determined their pros and cons as they relate to your house for rent, and estimated what your trade area or sphere of influence is with the house that you have.

- Eye-catching Signs are finished and a Property Flyer that provides just enough information to act as a hook and get the prospective renter to call has been designed.

- A Website has been launched that provides some basic information on the house, allows a prospect to view your lease requirements and to download a flyer and a rental application.

- Your Basic Property Presentation is prepared for when the calls do come in, scripted to repeat the rental information on your flyer and website, allowing you to pre-qualify the prospective renter and to set up a face-to-face meeting to view the house.

So far, so good.

But, Signs, Flyers, Website and Presentation are all passive activities. Their effectiveness depends on a prospective renter reaching out to you.

Signs depend on the renter driving around, the website depends on the renter surfing the Internet, and the presentation depends on the renter picking up the phone and calling you.

95% of rental house investors will stop at this point and hope that these passive activities to get their space leased.

With market conditions as they are now, where in many markets it's a renter's market, you've got to do more.

The top 5% develop active Multiple Marketing Messages for each property.

By identifying different target markets for the same available rental, then creating individual marketing messages or advertisements to reach each target market segment, the maximum exposure for the house you're trying to rent is reached.

In using your inexpensive on-line marketing channels to communicate multiple messages you'll be increasing the number of potential tenants seeing your message and will be proactively offering ideas for the use of your space.

Let your creative juices flow when creating Multiple Marketing Messages!

Let's take a step-by-step look.

Even though we're using a small four-unit apartment building in this example the same techniques can easily apply to a single-family rental home, condo or town home, as well as larger apartment buildings.

Multiple Marketing Messages for Apartments

Our four-unit apartment building has one 2-bed/1-bath 700 square foot unit available for rent.

Competitive research shows that the asking rent is mid-range for the overall market, making the unit very affordably priced. The rent includes all utilities except electric, and there is a detached storage room, and use of the common-area laundry room. The property also has a small grassy courtyard, and one assigned parking space for each unit, plus on-street parking.

The apartment building is located within walking distance of a community college and a large shopping center, the nearest public transit system stop is one block away, and the demographics in the immediate area around the building are considered lower income.

From this information we can develop five Multiple Marketing Messages for our vacant apartment.

These messages focus on:

1. Students attending the local community college
2. Affordable housing tenants
3. Amenities of the apartment - Free common-area laundry, grassy courtyard, detached storage unit
4. Small, quiet building - Positioning our four-unit building against the larger apartment complexes in the area
5. Public transit - Tenants can walk to shopping or restaurants, and easily take public transit to travel further

Create one individual advertisement for each selling point, or five different advertisements in all, and you'll quickly reach the highest number of prospective renters in the shortest period of time!

One note of caution: Be careful not to accidentally violate any fair housing laws that may be in force in your market when developing multiple marketing messages for residential property.

Do You Want To Get Paid? Then Close The Deal!

You've got your house for rent. Your basic marketing materials are in place. The basic property presentation provides just enough information to hook the prospective renter. You've asked enough open-ended questions of the renter to ensure that she can qualify for the house you have for rent.

All that's left is to meet the prospective renter face-to-face, do some final qualifying, set the hook, and sign the lease.

Basic Steps needed to Close The Deal

Showing the Rental House

Step #1: How you Present Yourself will Determine the Future Expectations & Behavior of the Tenant

In addition to evaluating the house to have for rent, renters will also evaluate you. Remember, they've got a lot to choose from, and just because your house made it to their short list doesn't mean they're ready to sign a lease just yet.

It's important to dress and act the part. Having done your competitive research and developed multiple marketing messages, you've already got a good idea of the types of renters you'll be dealing with.

Think about the profiles of the tenants you're attracting from your marketing and position yourself just one level above that.

They are your customers and you want the rental income, but ultimately you're also the landlord and property manager who will need to collect rents, enforce property rules & regulations, and possibly evict tenants.

Properly positioning yourself from the first meeting will make managing the rental house and the renter much easier in the long run.

Step #2: Repeat Yourself & Ask Questions

The renter was provided some basic information with your property flyer and website. Your basic property presentation repeated and added to that same basic information when the prospective renter called.

Now repeat that same basic information again when showing the house.

The prospective renter has probably looked at several locations and may not remember your flyer or what you said over the phone.

This is another opportunity to drive home the pros of your house for rent compared to the competition and to address any foreseeable questions & objections before they come up.

Use Open-Ended Questions again, but this time the objective is to Set the Hook!

You want to transition the prospect renter from thinking of your available space as an option to thinking of your space as the only option they have.

Here are some Examples of Open-Ended Questions to use:

"How well would your furniture fit in the living room?"
"Whose bedroom would this be?"
"When do you see yourself moving in?"
"What do you think about the floor plan?"
"Where do you live now?"

Develop at least 20 open-ended questions to ask when showing your rental.

Rotate them throughout your presentations with different prospective renters. Doing this will keep things interesting for you and will also let you discover which questions are the most effective in getting prospects to talk.

Remember, question starters are: Who, What, Where, When, Why and How.

Qualifying the Tenant

Throughout this eBook we've talked a lot about you putting your best foot forward with prospective tenants, but shouldn't they do the same for you?

Of course they should.

Part A: The First Date

Think of meeting a prospective tenant for the first time as if you're on a first date.

This is an excellent technique to use when meeting new prospects. It provides a great "reality check" with the prospect and goes a long way toward avoiding problem tenants.

The best behavior you're going to see from a tenant is the first time you meet them, before a lease is signed and they rent your house.

If the prospect is difficult to deal with, vague, disrespectful, if any other red flags arise, or if something just doesn't feel right, remember things will just get worse once they owe you rent money.

It's a lot easier taking a pass with this type of tenant and moving on to the next one, because after they sign a lease they'll be a lot harder to deal with or get rid of.

Part B: Schedule Showings During Normal Hours

This is another sure-fire qualifying technique to use with prospective tenants.

Think about the times you've looked for a place to rent. You were a serious prospect, so chances are you expected to set appointments to look during normal business hours.

Why would you expect anything less from a qualified tenant prospect for your house?

During your competitive research you probably checked out the nearby apartment buildings and noted their leasing office hours. If they have Monday - Friday 9 a.m. to 5 p.m. hours, with half a day on Saturday, and are closed on Sundays, then they're doing this for several reasons.

One of those reasons is to screen out unqualified tenants.

Beware of Tenants in a Hurry to Sign a Lease

If your house has been vacant for a while it's tempting to cut corners when a prospective renter wants to move in right away.

Be aware, if a tenant wants to sign a lease quickly it's a red flag.

The people renting your house will more than likely end up leaving as quickly as they wanted to move in and may vandalize the property as well.

Let's look at this real-life example:

"I Need to Move In Today!"

It's possible to complete the residential leasing process in one day, with steps including:

- Showing the property
- Receiving the completed rental application + support documents
- Checking references + verifying application information
- Running credit and background checks
- Verifying utility set-up
- Drawing up the lease and signing

Just because it is possible to do all of this the same day, it's best not to.

If the available unit has been vacant for some time or if you're a leasing agent or management company that wants to get space leased quickly for your client this recommendation is tough to take.

But think about the times when you or people you know have looked for a place to rent. Did they have to move in right away? Why? The answer is probably a red flag.

Rushing through the normal application process, or even worse, deciding to cut corners simply because the prospective tenants insists, sets a bad precedent with the tenant and guarantees there will be problems down the road.

Tenants that need to move in quickly will move out just as quickly, without notice, before their lease is up and you'll run a higher risk of the property being damaged as well.

Making It Legal - Applications & Leases

I've personally rented residential property for my own use and often times have never been asked to fill out an application. As long as the lease was signed and the money was in the bank, the property owner had no complaints.

Now maybe I just happen to look very legitimate, but my guess is that in these cases the property owner had either forgotten to bring an application form with him or just didn't see the need to use one since they'd never had a problem in the past.

Knock on wood.

Using an application form adds legitimacy to the leasing process in the mind of the tenant in the same way that using a lease containing a certain number of pages does.

"Legitimacy" means that the tenant will take the lease obligation more seriously.

Residential Lease Documents

On the new few pages you'll find samples of:

1. Residential Application. The rental requirements are customary for the market the property is located in, are prominently listed at the top of the application, and are applied equally to every applicant.
2. Move-in Checklist. This is the tenant's statement of the condition of the property when they moved in. The Checklist can be used for move-outs as well, and the two documents can be compared to assess any potential damages to the property.

3. Tenant Handbook. Used in conjunction with the lease. While the lease will cover general terms, the Handbook can be used to cover items that are specific to your rental house.

1234 S. North Avenue, City, State 90123

Phone: 310-123-4567　　Fax: 866-123-4567　　Email: Info@BasicPropertyManagement.com

Rental Application

☑ Anyone over the age of 18 intending to live in the property must fill out a separate rental application
☑ A non-refundable fee of $40 per person, cash or guaranteed funds, must accompany each application
☑ A legible, current copy of each applicant's driver's license or state issued photo ID must be attached
☑ Copies of your last four pay stubs, or if self-employed a copy of last year's tax return, must be attached
☑ We will contact prior landlords and references. Please make sure a valid phone number is provided
☑ If you need additional space please attach additional paper
☑ Your earnest money deposit to hold the property is due within 24 hours of application approval

Property address: _____

Desired date of occupancy: _____

Reason for moving: _____

Applicant Information

Name: _____

Social security number: _____

Date of birth: _____

Home phone: _____ Work phone: _____ Cell phone: _____

Residence History

Current rent/mortgage payment (monthly): _____

Current address: _____

City: _____ State: _____ Zip: _____

How long at this address?: _____

Landlord name and phone number: _____

Previous address: _____

City: _____ State: _____ Zip: _____

Landlord name and phone number: _____

How long at this address?: _____

Reason for moving to current address?: _____

Employment, Bank and References

Current Employer: _____ Phone: _____

Address/City/State/Zip: _____

Position: _____ How long?: _____

Monthly gross income: _____

Name of contact to verify employment: _____

Previous Employer: _____ Phone: _____

Address/City/State/Zip: _____

Position: _____ How long?: _____

Monthly gross income: _____

Name of contact to verify employment: _____

Bank name: _____ Branch/Phone: _____

Checking account #: _____ Savings account #: _____

Other income, from where and how much?: _____
                                    (Please attach documentation to prove this)

Personal reference name: _____

Address/City/State/Zip: _____

Phone: _____ Relationship: _____

Emergency contact name: _____

Address/City/State/Zip: _____

Phone: _____ Relationship: _____

Debt Obligations

Total outstanding debt: $ _____ *(Include credit card, car loans, personal loans, etc.)*

Total monthly debt payments: $ _____

Monthly payments for: Alimony: $_____ Child support: $_____ Other: $_____

Do you have any tax liens? If 'yes', explain: _____

Have you ever filed for bankruptcy? If 'yes', explain: _____

Have you or anyone who will be occupying the property plea bargained or been convicted of any felony or misdemeanor? If 'yes', explain: _____

Vehicle Information

Driver's license #: _____ State: _____ Expires: _____

Vehicles you own, drive, or will be parking at the property: *(Include make, model, year and plate number)*

1. _____

2. _____

3. _____

Children and/or Additional Occupants

Please list the full names, ages, and relationship of all people who will be occupying the property:

1. _____

2. _____

3. _____

4. _____

5. _____

6. _____

☑ I understand that a $40 application fee, by cash or guaranteed funds, must be included with this application and that it is not refundable

☑ I understand that a legible copy of a driver's license or state issued ID, and any other documentation noted herein, must be included with this application

☑ I hereby warrant that the above information is true and correct and I authorize the person or firm to whom this application is made to obtain credit, reference, and other investigative information from the sources herein and shall release and harmless said person or firm from liability for any damages that may result from furnishing this information to its owners, agents or others

☑ If for any reason any information provided in this application is later found to be false I understand that the lease may be declared null and void and that immediate eviction may begin

☑ This application is subject to acceptance and execution of a rental agreement and is offered without respect to race, creed, color, sex, national origin or family status

_____

Applicant's name, printed

_____   _____

Applicant's signature   Date

"Move In Inspection Form"

Property ddress: _____
TenantName: _____ Occupancy Date: _____
Phone Numbers; hm. _____ wk. _____

This form is to be completed by the tenant following the occupancy of their rental property. It is not to be used as a repair work order form. Please include in this form the general condition of the property when you took occupancy. You may be as specific as you wish. If you need to utilize additional paper, please do so. This form will be reviewed at the time that you vacate the property in order to document condition of the property when you moved in. Must be returned to management within 2 weeks of occupancy.

Kitchen/Dining Area:
Stove. Oven and Microwave: _____
Dishwasher and Disposal: _____
Refrigerator: _____
Floor Coverings: _____
Walls and Cabinets. _____
Counters and Sinks: _____
Window Coverings: _____
Windows and Screens: _____
Doors and Locks: _____

Living Room Area:
Walls and Ceilings: _____
Floor Coverings: _____
Lights and Fixtures: _____
Window Coverings: _____
Windows and Screens: _____
Doors and Locks: _____

Den/Family Room:
Walls and Ceilings: _____
Floor Coverings: _____
Lights and Fixtures: _____
Window Coverings: _____
Windows and Screens: _____
Doors and Locks: _____

Bathrooms and Laundry:
Walls and Ceilings: _____
Floor Coverings: _____
Lights and Fixtures: _____
Windows and Screens: _____
Doors and Locks: _____
Toilets and Sinks: _____
Showers and Cabinets: _____
Plumbing Fixtures: _____

Bedroom #1 or Mst. Bedroom:
Walls and Ceilings:_____
Floor Coverings:_____
Lights and Fixtures:_____
Window Coverings:_____
Windows and Screens:_____
Doors and Locks:_____

Bedroom #2:
Walls and Ceilings:_____
Floor Coverings:_____
Lights and Fixtures:_____
Window Coverings:_____
Windows and Screens:_____
Doors and Locks:_____

Bedroom #3:
Walls and Ceilings:_____
Floor Coverings:_____
Lights and Fixtures:_____
Window Coverings:_____
Windows and Screens:_____
Doors and Locks:_____

Carports, Garages, Storage Rooms and Patios:
Walls and Ceilings:_____
Doors and Locks:_____
Lights and Fixtures:_____

Cooling, Heating and Water Heaters:
Air Conditioning or Evaporative Cooling:_____
Heating Systems:_____
Thermostats and A/C Filters:_____
Hot Water Heating Systems:_____
Smoke Alarm Systems:_____

Yards and Lawns:
Front Lawns:_____
Rear Lawn, patio or balcony:_____
Plants and Trees:_____
Irrigation or Sprinkler Systems:_____

Other:_____
_____
_____
_____

Tenant Signature:_____ **Date:**_____

Management CoSignature:_____ **Date:**_____

32

TENANT HANDBOOK AND RENTAL POLICIES

This Handbook and Policies is an Addendum to your lease. If there is a conflict in language between this Addendum and your Lease, then this Addendum shall prevail.

Rent

Rent must be received at the address stated in your lease and is due in advance on or before the first of every month. We do not accept cash. If you payment is dishonored for any reason, late charges and service charges will be added to your account as provided for in your lease, and we will require that any future payments be made by guaranteed funds.

Renters Insurance

You are required to maintain renter's insurance during the term of your lease and any renewal thereof. The insurance shall be issued by a licensed insurance company of your choice and shall provide limits of not less than $50,000 per occurrence. Proof of insurance shall be provided prior to possession of the property. If you fail to obtain or maintain this insurance you shall be in default of your lease.

CC&Rs/HOAs

These are rules and regulations set forth by the Homeowner's Association. If there are CC&R's for your property you will receive a copy of them as part of your lease. Please read them thoroughly as you will be required to obey all of the rules and regulations. Any fines that we are charged by the HOA for your not obeying these regulations will be assessed to you, and will be considered additional rent. You will face eviction from the property if these fines are not paid or if HOA violations are continuous.

Emergencies

If you ever encounter an emergency day or night, always call 911 or other professional emergency personnel first. Then, if possible, contact our office.

Keys and Locks

At the time of possession of the property you were provided with keys and garage door openers as stated in your lease. If you lock yourself out of the property it is your responsibility, at your expense, to call a locksmith for service. Changing or altering any lock is prohibited without our express written permission.

Dogs, Cats and Other Pets

Unless provided for in your lease pets are not allowed at the property you are renting. If you wish to acquire a pet after you begin your lease, please contact us for prior approval, to pay the appropriate fees and to sign additional lease documentation. We reserve the right to prohibit pets that we believe, in our sole discretion, are a breed, cross breed or related to a pit bull, rottweiler or Cane Carso.

Your initials: _____ _____ _____ _____

33

Access

Except in the case of an emergency we will not enter your property without prior notice. We do reserve the right to conduct periodic semi-annual surveys, for which prior notice will be given.

A/C Units, Heating Units, Smoke Detectors

All filters must be replaced one a month. Any damage to the heating or cooling units that are a result of your not replacing the filters every month will be charged to you, and will be considered additional rent. Smoke detectors should be checked by you at least twice a year.

Extermination/Pest Control/Weed Control/Landscaping

You must report any pest or weed problems to us within two weeks of your move in. Any pest infestations or weed growth after that time will be your responsibility to treat, at your expense. You will be responsible for maintaining the landscaping around your property after you move in.

Home Warranty/General Maintenance

You are expected to maintain your property with reasonable care, so that the property is returned to us in the condition that you rented it in. If your property has a home warranty on it, you will be responsible for the service call fee on all covered repairs up to the amount of the repair deductible. You will be provided with the warranty name, phone number and contact number when you move in. You will be held responsible for any damage to the property or its systems that is due to your misuse or abuse. If you are unsure of how to maintain part of the property or its systems it is your responsibility to ask us for assistance. Property systems include, but are not limited to: air conditioning and heating, plumbing, electrical, lighting, walls and ceilings, flooring, appliances, doors and windows, and garage door opener. You are liable for a mechanical failure of any of the systems if the failure was caused by your abuse or neglect.

Unauthorized Repair Charges

Except as provided for in the Arizona Residential Landlord Tenant Act you are prohibited from making unauthorized repairs to the property or its systems and deducting such charges from your rent.

Vehicles

Non-operative and unlicensed vehicles are not permitted on the property. Major mechanical repair work on vehicles is not permitted on premises. Commercial vehicles may not be parked on premises without our prior written permission.

Abandoned Property

You agree that if any of your belongings are left at the property after you vacate, then we will consider it abandoned and we will remove or destroy it at our sole discretion.

Move-out Notice/Inspection

You must provide us with a 30-day written notice of your intent to move out, even if your lease is ending. It is your responsibility to schedule your move-out inspection with us. Inspections are to be scheduled in advance and take place during normal weekday business hours only.

Your initials: _____ _____ _____ _____

In addition to the tenant completing and signing the Application, the supporting documents asked for are a legible government issued photo identification and proof of income. Provable income means verifiable recent pay stubs or a history of bank deposits.

Make sure not to accidentally ask questions that violate any fair housing laws in the municipality that you operate in when developing your rental application.

Finding The Actual Lease

The actual lease you use for your rental house will vary from market to market.

Experienced real estate investors don't write a lease from scratch. Why reinvent the wheel when there are plenty of free or inexpensive alternatives available?

Here are The Top Five ways to make sure that your Application, Lease and Lease Documents are in-line with the customs of the market you're operating in:

#1: Search On-line for local Property Management Companies

Many times their application forms or leases can be downloaded and can serve as a guideline for the application you create.

#2: Personally visit Apartment Buildings in your market area

Ask for an application and sample lease to take with you. Conducting an on-line search may work almost as well.

#3: Interview local Leasing Agents & Property Management Companies

Ask for samples of the forms that they use. You may find a leasing agent that you like and trust, and decide to contract with her to save you the time and trouble of dealing with prospective tenants.

#4: Check with the Evictions Attorney you selected when you were identifying your Vendors

Ask them to provide or recommend applications, leases and addenda. Many will have these available for download from their websites at no charge.

#5: Make use of Inexpensive On-line Services

Good resources are FindLegalForms.com, EZLandlordforms.com or OnLineForms.LawDepot.com. Select the municipality your property is located in and for a few dollars you have a fill-in-the-blank lease to use.

Service After The Sale - How to Find and Keep Good Vendors

In this section we'll discuss the vendors needed for any income producing property, where to find them, and how to keep them.

We'll also discuss ways to use your vendors to stay on top of the competition, how to use your vendors to gather information to improve management of the property, and how your selected vendors can send the right or wrong signals to your tenants.

Let's begin with a real-life example that shows how using the wrong vendors for the wrong tasks can send the wrong message to your tenants.

When tenants begin to question their landlord's management skills, business ability, and financial strength the result will be an increase in slow payment on rents, increased repair requests and an increase in tenant turnover – meaning less income & more expenses for the rental house.

The Spray Painted Bathtub

How maintenance work is performed in residential property, especially when the tenant is present, plays a critical role in tenant satisfaction and in avoiding complaints to the local housing authorities or, worst case, a potential lawsuit.

My company worked briefly - very briefly - with the owner of a portfolio of several single-family residential properties who decided to try and save money by hiring a relative to do maintenance work.

A single mother with a two-year old was the tenant in one of the rental homes, and noticed that the finish on her bathtub had begun to peel. She submitted a service request to the owner to have the tub repaired.

After several days, the owner sent his relative over to the house. To save money, the owner instructed the relative to selectively spray paint the areas of the bathtub that were peeling. So now the tenant with the two-year old had a tub with two different colors - one the original finish and the other the spray paint.

After being used a few times the tub began peeling again, only this time it was the spray paint that was peeling.

I can only guess at how this story ended, because when we learned of this repair we immediately terminated our relationship with the property owner. It's mind boggling that the repair was done in this manner, but it's absolutely true.

Profit margins in single-family rental property can be razor thin, especially if the property is leveraged, and every dollar saved drops straight to the bottom line. But if doing this type of repair to save a few dollars results in losing a tenant because she's not happy, then much more is lost than saved.

With many residential rental homes that are leveraged with mortgages, the loss of only one month of rental income can easily wipe out a year's worth of profit from the property!

Your 30 Must-Have Vendors List

There are 30 must-have vendors you'll need for the management of any investment property:

1. Handyman
2. Landscaper
3. Pest Control & Termite
4. Locksmith

5. Glass Company
6. HVAC Company
7. Plumber
8. Electrician
9. Sign Company
10. Waste Disposal
11. Debris Removal
12. Roofing Company
13. Insurance Agent
14. Post Installation Company
15. Surveyor
16. Flooring Company
17. Carpet Cleaner
18. Printer
19. Towing Company
20. Appliance Sales & Service
21. Alarm Monitoring
22. Cleaning Company
23. Parking Lot Sweeper
24. Collections Service
25. Tree Service
26. Swimming Pool Company
27. Garage Door Company
28. Parking Lot Paving & Striping
29. Telecommunications Company
30. Painter

Many investors will use the services of an accountant for filing year-end tax returns and any monthly use or sales tax returns.

Professional investors also find it helpful to maintain contact with an attorney, preferably keeping one on retainer.

- For Residential Property you'll want to have an attorney who specializes in evictions and judgments and who can guide you through the process.

What to Look for in a Vendor

Here are The Top Four Things we look for in Vendors that we want to keep giving repeat business to:

1. Vendors who are competitively priced but not necessarily the cheapest

The cheapest vendors are the ones most likely to disappear the next time you need them. When we contact a vendor we want to know that we are getting a fair price without having to go out to bid each time that, say, a broken piece of window glass needs to be replaced or a lock needs to be picked.

2. Vendors who are up-front about their abilities and schedule

We want to know that when we call the vendor for a repair, they'll respond quickly and will be able to do the job properly. It does no good to call a handyman to make a plumbing repair only to discover that he really can't handle copper pipe work, during which time water is leaking into the tenant's suite or apartment.

3. Vendors who are up-front with their fees and who present itemized billing

The intent is not to nickel-and-dime but to know what we're being charged for. Recently we received a lump-sum invoice from a plumber for work done in clearing a drain line. We called and had them re-submit an invoice that itemized the work that was done.

This wasn't a delaying tactic to avoid paying the bill. Not getting an itemized invoice makes it difficult to compare rates from previous similar jobs done or from alternative vendors.

Frequently the first time we use a vendor for a job they'll discount the project without telling us. We appreciate that, but we always ask up front what their normal fee is. Doing so sets the proper expectations going forward and lets us know if we're comparing apples to apples right from the start.

There are going to be some cases where itemized billing doesn't always make sense. Weekly landscaping, changing a door handle or cleaning a carpet are all good examples. We've seen some investors insist on an itemized invoice for every job, big or small. While they do get their detailed statement, they also have a high turnover rate with the vendors that do the small jobs.

4. We look for vendors of professional services whose way of doing business is a match for the property owner

Choosing an attorney is an excellent example of this. Many of the investors my company works with are private individuals with property owned under an LLC or S-Corp.

When choosing a professional services vendor such as an attorney, we look for a certain comfort and trust level, along with an attorney whose practice is a close match for the property owner.

For example, an insurance company that owns a trophy Class A apartment building is going to want legal advice from a large multi-partner law firm with regional or national exposure, whereas an individual investor will be more comfortable dealing with a sole practitioner.

Also, an attorney in private practice will probably work harder for you than will a large law firm that you represent less potential business to.

How to Keep Vendors

There are Three Ways to Keep Good Vendors:

#1: Be up-front about your expectations

This makes everybody more comfortable and reduces the chance of there being issues when the job is done or complaints from the tenant about shoddy work.

#2: Pay promptly

If the payment term for the job is net 30, pay net 15. If you're sent an invoice and the payment term is COD, pay that day.

Some property owners feel that if they are under duress due to a high vacancy level, that everyone should "feel their pain". Problem is, it doesn't work that way, and the next time there's a water leak in an apartment they'll find their calls to the plumber that they slow paid are not being returned.

#3: Give them as much work as possible

It's better to have a few reliable, responsive vendors than to shop each and every job around trying to find that new customer discount. You'll get a faster response and better pricing when the vendor knows they're your go-to guy and that you'll pay promptly.

Where to Find Good Vendors

People tend to associate with people like themselves. With that in mind, here are The Top Three Ways to Find Vendors worth keeping:

#1: For attorneys and accountants conduct face-to-face interviews

We've had good luck finding attorneys and accountants using Craigslist and professional trade magazines, along with Internet searches for a specific type of practice. Most are happy to take a little time and meet with potential clients, explain their practice and how their fees work. If they're too busy to do this, move on to your next choice.

You're also able to explain your situation in detail and set the right expectations, along with discussing any projected projects.

One thing we do not look for with a professional service vendor is a personality match.

Do you really want to seek out an accountant who is prone to practical jokes, just because you are?

#2: Referrals from existing vendors

Once you've established a good relationship with a vendor, odds are they're going to know others that can assist you.

It's surprising how many trade referrals you can get from one or two vendors that work well for you. For example, from one air conditioning vendor we've received excellent referrals for electricians and plumbers.

The first time we engage a vendor we'll meet them on-site at the property, and have a face-to-face talk about what we look for, the possibility of future work, and what their areas of expertise are, so that everyone starts off on the right foot.

We also want to gauge what impression the vendor is going to make on the tenants.

Going forward, we may not always meet them in person when there are additional jobs, but we know that the project will be dependably done and the pricing will be fair.

#3: Prospecting the neighborhood

This works well for finding landscapers, plumbers and handymen, who tend to only work in one part of town or another. We'll drive around the immediate area where our property is located and look for vendors in the middle of a project, then see if they don't mind being interrupted to talk about our property just down the street.

With this method it's also easier to contact the neighbor they were doing the work for to check for customer satisfaction. We've found very good carpet cleaners and landscapers using this method.

A very important benefit of using the same vendors is that, over time, you'll be able to use them as a resource for gathering information to improve the management of your property.

Are You Really Making Money? - Tracking Income & Expenses

I've seen very astute professional real estate investors use various methods to track and report their income and expenses of an investment property.

Some use customized subscription based software, some will develop their own spreadsheet to track performance, and some will use off-the-shelf software such as QuickBooks or QuickBooks Pro.

Regardless of the system selected, there are several pieces of information that any basic bookkeeping system should provide.

Most of the investors we work use a cash accounting system instead of an accrual system. With cash accounting you're booking rents when they are received and bills when they are paid.

Since this is 'real time' accounting, your profit & loss statement ends up being your cash flow statement as well, which suits most investors just fine.

If you're not sure which is best for you check with an accountant. Remember to review Chapter 4 for suggestions on how to find a good accountant and other vendors.

Profit & Loss Statements

Here's a sample Profit & Loss (P&L) statement for a single-family residential rental property.

The line items for other property types will be similar to what you see here.

Basic Property Management Account
Profit and Loss Standard
January through December 20XX

	Jan - Dec 'XX
Ordinary Income/Expense	
Income	
Fee Income	142.84
Rental	9,189.43
Total Income	9,332.27
Expense	
HOA fees	216.00
Lease Commission	396.00
Licenses and Permits	87.00
Management Fees	600.00
Miscellaneous	30.00
Postage and Delivery	19.40
Repairs	
Building Repairs	609.14
Repairs - Other	1,522.00
Total Repairs	2,131.14
Taxes	
Local	224.91
Total Taxes	224.91
Utilities	
Landscape	415.00
Pool maintenance	178.00
Water	383.98
Total Utilities	976.98
Total Expense	4,681.43
Net Ordinary Income	4,650.84
Net Income	4,650.84

With cash accounting your P&L ends up being your cash flow statement.

You'll also want to keep track of your receivables, in this case the rents due from tenants or deposits you may have made for utilities, and to have a system to ensure that your payables, or bills due to vendors, don't sneak up on you.

This can often be something as simple as notes in your computerized calendar.

Five Bookkeeping Must Haves

In addition to the basic P&L line items in our example, there are Five More Items we expect any Bookkeeping System to provide:

Item #1 - Rent Statements

Even if you don't send monthly rent statements it's a good idea to have a system than can generate them if needed, for a couple of reasons:

- It's easier to track miscellaneous fees such as late charges, rent credits, and NSF fees

- Professionally printed statements that show a history of charges and payments carry more weight if you ever have to evict a tenant and go to court to obtain a judgment to collect unpaid rent

Item #2 - Balance Sheet

The balance sheet should provide information such as:

- Tenant deposits that may be refundable

- Utility deposits that you may have paid that are owed to you

- Accounts receivable showing the aging of the amounts that tenants owe you

Item #3 - Bank Account Reconciliation

Provide a quick way to balance the operating bank account for the property every month.

Item #4 - Monthly & Annual Reports

There are several reasons to have professional, clean looking financial statements, even if you own the property free & clear and you don't have any partners:

- New Owner. At some point the property will be sold. Having clean, professional financial reports will go a long way toward satisfying your buyer that the financial performance is genuine.

- Tax Purposes. You may be audited for rental or use tax payments. Your accountant, CPA or bookkeeper may need legible reports. The Government may need legible reports. As with your potential buyer, the same can be said that having clean reports will help to get any tax or return issues resolved much quicker.

- Lender. Having professional reports will assure your lender that its money is not at risk and that a loan has been made to an astute real estate investor. If you're selling the property, the buyer's bank as well as the buyer will appreciate "clean" reports that could make the difference between the deal closing or not closing.

Item #5 - Budget

Use the budget to track actual performance to expectations, and to provide a quick glance at which tenants are current and which are not.

If you've got a single-tenant property or don't have partners then having a budget may not be much of a concern, since you probably have a good intuitive feel for how the property is performing.

On the other hand, if you're looking for a loan, trying to pull cash out of the property, or trying to convince a potential buyer to make an offer, if your budget can show that you're beating expectations, this historical performance can make an excellent sales tool.

Now that we know what type of financial information we need, how do we get it?

Accounting Software

For single-tenant properties or smaller multi-tenant properties QuickBooks Pro is our favorite. This software is off-the-shelf, and allows you to set up multiple properties and multiple companies.

We've used QuickBooks Pro to manage multiple properties with over 20 tenants each. Everything we look for in a basic bookkeeping system is available, and as long as you have some basic financial training, or know someone that does, the software is very easy to use.

Investors that own larger multi-tenant properties may find that software specific to their property type makes more sense. Yardi and Rent Manager are a couple of examples.

Bigger multi-tenant property typically has a higher tenant turnover, and with a larger number of individual units, tracking individual deposits, receivables, turnover and unit-specific repair costs becomes more of a challenge. The reporting format is also geared toward multiple owners of a single property, so providing consolidated snap shot reports may be a little easier with property-type specific software.

Keep in mind that customized software is normally subscription based and that the data may not be easily transferable to another system should you decide to change. You may find yourself being locked into software that down the road ends up not suiting your needs.

Investment Real Estate Analysis

A Case Study

by

Jeffrey Roark

Author of *The Real Estate Property Management Guide*

Overview

It's a well kept secret in buying investment real estate that you are almost always buying the seller's problem.

Think about it this way: If a property has good tenants, is for the most part trouble-free and is cash flowing, why on earth would the current owner want to sell? Sure, there are some legitimate reasons, but even those innocent sounding excuses for selling can hide a hidden agenda. It's safe to say that 99% of the time the new owner is going to face problems with their property purchase, probably sooner rather than later.

Now, the fact that problems may exist doesn't mean an investor shouldn't buy a property. For example, let's say the current use for a building is a multi-tenant office property with a high vacancy rate and you (as the buyer) want to turn it into offices for your business. Or an apartment building needs significant capital improvements, such as a roof repair or replacement of a majority of the HVAC units. Or a retail property sits very close to a school or to a church, a situation that current zoning laws may prohibit your leasing to certain types of tenants, thereby reducing the number of potential business types you can market your vacant retail suites to.

The key is to accurately identify the existing and potential problems, and the likely costs associated with solving those problems. In *The Real Estate Property Management Guide* I discuss all aspects of property management, including the steps to take when considering what type of investment property is right for you. After all, just because you can buy or finance an acquisition doesn't mean that you should actually invest in it.

In this book, *Investment Real Estate Analysis: A Case Study*, we drill-down on the specific analysis used by all professional investment real estate brokers and buyers to determine the strengths and weaknesses - and to identify the hidden opportunities - when deciding how to position a piece of real estate for sale. While this case study is written from the seller perspective, as a potential buyer you should *always* apply these same steps yourself to gain a thorough understanding of what you are buying - before you sign the purchase contract!

This case study is based on an actual activity and will take you inside the mind of a professional real estate investor. While the property type being analyzed is a single-tenant, free-standing office building and while the specific pricing recommendations may not apply to your market or property, the same techniques can be used for any income producing or owner-occupied real estate.

So, enough talk, let's dig into the analysis!

The Activity

The property is a 3,680 square foot, single tenant, free standing building located in the South Scottsland/Northdale sub-market of the City.

The building had been gutted and completely re-built by the owner in three years ago as a single story owner-occupied medical office facility with eight parking spaces and pole signage with excellent visibility from the freeway. The property faces Scotts Road, a major north-south route between Scottsland and Tempdale and is approximately ¼ mile from the freeway on-off ramp. Zoning for the property allows office use, limited retail, and light manufacturing, distribution and automotive uses.

One year after re-building the property the owner of the building exited the City marketplace and began unsuccessful efforts to market the vacant property for sale. In July, after meeting with the CEO and the VP of Operations for the owner, I agreed to list the property for sale as the exclusive agent.

My client's objective was to sell the property but they were willing to consider intermediate steps – such as leasing the vacant property – that would ultimately help to maximize the resale value of the property.

Property Overview

The property sits in a dense, high-growth area. Within two miles to the south is the University, the Lakefront mixed-use developments, and the Marketplace, a new 1.3 million square foot retail development. Within a few miles to the north of the property are the redeveloping areas of South Scottsland and the 1.2 million square foot University Center for Technology, an office/retail park.

While the property had several positives there were also a few obstacles to marketing the property:

1. Parking – Typical office parking ratios in the market are around 3-4:1000 square feet. This property offered a ratio of about 2.2:1000. No alternative or "over flow" space was available so the target market of prospective office users for the space was narrowed to those that did not need much day-long parking for employees.

2. Vacant Building – When I began marketing the property for sale in the Fall demand from investors for income producing property was very strong but few at that time were willing to take the risk of purchasing a vacant building and then leasing it. However, by the following Spring product scarcity and demand had reached the point where investors now were willing to do this, and this is ultimately who the property was sold to.

3. Days on Market – The owners had tried for over a year to sell the property on their own, and through another broker, at a price of $900,000. I advised my client that since the property had sat on the market for so long prospective buyers and their brokers familiar with the market were bound to sense a distress sale and to price their offers accordingly. This did indeed happen as described below.

Courses of Action & Recommendations

The sales comparison approach was used to calculate the asking list price of $650,000 for the property.

A lease analysis was conducted and a rate of $16 modified gross was established and a pro forma APOD (annual property operating data report) was prepared to illustrate to the client the estimated resale range of $730,000 - $780,000 based on market CAP rates of 7.5% - 8% if the property could be positioned as an income producing property.

[**CAP rate** stands for Capitalization Rate, which is the ratio between the annual net cash income of a property (before debt service and the non-cash expenses of amortization and depreciation) and the value of the property. For example, a property with an NOI - net operating income - of $100,000 and an asset value of $1,000,000 would have a CAP rate of 10%.]

A ground lease analysis was also conducted and reviewed with the client. (This analysis is also explained in detail under Analysis and Computations, but was discounted as a marketing approach due to the perceived complexity of ground leasing by the client.)

[Often written for 100 years, a **ground lease** allows the seller to retain rights to the land while the buyer may build on and improve the property for their own use, usually with certain covenants and restrictions. When the lease expires it is either re-negotiated and renewed, or the buyer is required to remove any improvements and the use of the land reverts back to the seller. Ground leasing is used in sub-markets where land is scarce and in high-demand. While there are certain attractions to ground leasing, at least from a seller perspective, that are definite negatives as well, as I discuss in the Analysis and Computations section of this book.]

The idea of dividing the space to create a multi-tenant property (which would have made the property more attractive to an investor), was reviewed with the client, but was discounted due to the limited parking and lot size.

Given the market demand and limitations of the property, the two best target markets for the property were identified as (1) Owner-users of office space and (2) Investors of income property.

My recommendation to the client was to simultaneously market the property for sale and for lease, with the understanding that if the property were leased first there would likely be a 6 to 12-month holding period needed to 'season' the tenant before the property could be put back on the market for sale.

This simultaneous approach was accepted by the VP of Operations but rejected by the CEO, so the property was marketed as a vacant owner-user or investor building.

Marketing Period

The marketing period ran from the Fall to the following Summer. During that time I received several offers to purchase in the $350,000 - $400,000 price range from owner-users looking for office/warehouse space. The prospective buyers were pricing into their offers the cost of renovation to suit their needs, the transitional nature of the area, and in some cases sensed a distress sale. The client declined these offers.

Although the property was not being marketed for lease, about 50% of the inquiries I received were from parties interested in leasing and I did receive several unsolicited offers to lease in the range of $15 to $16.50 per square foot which rationalized the lease analysis that was conducted when listing the property for sale. These offers to lease were declined by the client.

About mid-way through the marketing period I became aware of an employment conflict between the VP of Operations and the CEO. As a result of this conflict the VP of Operations, whose family had privately financed the purchase of the property, was calling the note due on the building and threatening foreclosure. The CEO instructed me that a quick sale was needed, preferably from a cash buyer with few contingencies.

Fortunately during the first two quarters of the new year the amount of speculative activity in the market continued to increase and over the next 90 days I was able to obtain six offers to purchase from prospective buyers. A $475,000 offer from an investor that met my client's terms and conditions was accepted and the transaction closed as scheduled.

While the recommendation to lease and then sell was not accepted by my client, the lease analysis and APOD were instrumental in obtaining the right offer from the right buyer.

I am now the leasing agent for the property, and we are currently in lease negotiations with the owner of a mortgage and alarm installation business. The prospective tenant is an established business relocating from a smaller facility, will require minimal TI (tenant improvements), and will provide the new owner of the building with stable rental income or the ability to re-sell the property as an income producing opportunity.

Site Analysis

The property is a 3,680 square foot, single tenant, free standing building sited on a 9,975 square foot lot located in the South Scottsland/North Tempdale sub-market of the City.

Zoning is I-2 industrial. This zoning classification allows for a wide variety of uses, including office, light industrial and distribution, automotive use, and limited retail use.

The lot is 100' x 100', fully improved with asphalt paving, sidewalks, gutters, desert landscaping and designated parking for eight vehicles.

There is 100' of frontage on Scottsland Road, which is a main north-south route between Tempdale and Scottsland. Traffic counts run 100,000 vehicles per day in front of the building. There is a large pole sign on the property.

All utility and municipal services are to the building, including electric, telephone, cable, water and sewer, and police and fire protection.

The building was originally built 45 years ago and was operated by a veterinarian until four years ago. At that time the building was gutted and completely remodeled by the current owner, including:

Electrical
Plumbing
Roofing - (foam roof)
4 HVAC units
Exterior wall refinishing

Interior completely reconfigured with reception, front office, conference room, multiple offices,

3 ADA-compliant restrooms
Security and fire alarm system
Smoke detectors
Phone system
DSL wired throughout
Music/intercom system

Ownership is fee simple.

Skills & Knowledge

The following is a list of the various areas of knowledge and expertise used when conducting this analysis:

1. Types of Real Estate Markets – Space market, Capital market, Property value market:

Marketing the vacant building to owner-users involved knowledge of competitive buildings sold or available for sale or lease and knowledge of neighborhood and regional development patterns.

Marketing the building to investors, who would then be seeking tenants, also involved knowledge of the Space market. This also required knowledge of operating costs, building-specific issues such as zoning and neighborhood growth projections to aid in development of an APOD, and comparison to other CAP rates available in the market from currently leased investment opportunities.

2. Comparing individual Office buildings:

Analysis of building data, rental data and community services was used in setting the listing price of the building, in the presentation to the client, and in the development of marketing materials for the property.

3. Alternative leasing strategies:

Although ultimately done as an exercise, ground leasing was examined as an alternative marketing and pricing strategy for the property.

4. Net Operating Income analysis:

Net operating income analysis was used in the development of the APOD for the property. Doing so required calculation of projected lease income and operating expenses.

5. Appraisal - Sales comparison approach to market value:

Because of the long-term vacancy of the property and the highest-and-best use challenges this approach was used to establish the listing price of the property. A survey of similar properties that had recently sold and those that were on the market for sale within a 5-mile radius of the subject was conducted and a pricing adjustment was made to factor in the property issues already discussed.

6. Appraisal - Income approach to market value:

Although this was not used to establish the listing price of the property, it was used as part of the pricing and marketing recommendations to the client, and in the APOD as part of the presentation material to income investors.

7. Perspectives of the User and the Investor:

Both owner-users and income investors were identified as likely buyers for the property. So, as part of the market analysis and marketing of the property the views of both sets of prospective buyers were considered.

8. Market Analysis Model:

The Trade Area and Income and Expenses portions of this model was used in developing the presentation materials, linkage analysis, neighborhood and regional analysis, and the APOD.

9. Market Research – Demographic/Economic and Property Data:

Extensive use was made of free and premium resources to obtain demographic and economic data. The current owner and the county assessor's office were used for property data.

10. Trade Area Gap Analysis:

The specific use and delineation of service area components of the Gap Analysis were identified through the market research above, and used to identify prospective owner-user categories for the property and to identify prospective tenants for the property when presenting to income investors.

11. Location and Site Feasibility:

The physical and regulatory limitations of the property were considered in determining the highest and best use of the existing improvements, identifying and marketing to prospective buyers, with the lease survey and development of the APOD. Demographic and economic data from free and premium resources and from the city of Scottsland and Tempdale municipal offices was also utilized.

12. Office market analysis:

This analysis was used to identify local owner-users of the property and to identify local prospective tenants for income investors. In conjunction with this, data mentioned in #11 above was used to determine the likely radius of the service area.

13. Applications to Investor Representation:

The value range was identified through the market data approach and through the income approach.

The property and market conditions were considered in determining the listing price; the pro forma lease rate and CAP rate range. Buyer appeal was also considered, as there were some very strong pluses and minuses to the property. Ultimately the client's motivation, specifically unwillingness to lease the property before sale and also the threat of foreclosure by the VP of Operations, determined the final sales price of the property.

The market data approach was used to determine the listing price of the building. A sales survey was conducted to identify comparable properties. As part of the presentation materials to income investors the income approach was used in development of the APOD to demonstrate the value of the property as a leased income investment.

Outline Of Assumptions

The following is a list of the assumptions made in this analysis:

1. Leasing up the property to maximize resale value:

From the 3rd quarter of the first year through the 1st quarter of the second year there was strong demand in the market from investors for multi-tenant income producing property, and secondarily for single-tenant income producing property. These fully leased properties were demanding CAP rates of around 7%.

For the subject property's APOD an estimated CAP rate of 7.5% - 8% was used, in part to reflect the additional risk an investor was taking by purchasing a single-tenant building with a newer tenant.

2. Highest and best use as flex office/warehouse:

While the building is located in an area with many mixed-use, high-density projects in planning or underway, it is in an unincorporated area of the County and the majority of the immediate neighboring property uses include fast food, printing, auto and auto parts sales, office/warehouse space, massage parlors and adult entertainment.

The first part of the marketing period illustrated the market perception of the best use of the building, with numerous offers received from buyers looking for flex space.

3. Use of sales comparison to set purchase price:

Prior to listing with me the owner had the property on the market for over a year, with the asking price set using the income approach. While this tactic sometimes worked short-term with the market conditions at the time, demand at the time was not so strong that this valuation approach could continue for over one year.

As the property was vacant for over a year, and had previously been occupied by the owner, the sales comparison approach was the most rational method to set an asking price. However, the APOD and lease analysis were used as marketing tools to justify the asking price and in presentations to interested investors.

4. $16 per square foot for APOD use:

This was obtained through a lease survey conducted in the immediate area, the details of which are in Analysis and Computations.

During the marketing period I received several unsolicited offers to lease in the range of $15 - $16.50 per square foot, which gave market support to the lease analysis.

5. Estimated six-month to one-year hold to season if leased before resale:

This estimated hold time was set after discussions with local lenders who required a minimum occupancy time by the tenant before offering financing to an investor.

The hold time was also based on observed demand in the market and the willingness of investors to accept the risk of a newly-occupied single tenant building. The higher than market CAP rate of 7.5% - 8% in the APOD also reflects this risk.

Analysis & Computations

The following is a list of the various steps and approaches used to analyze the property:

Sales Comparison Approach

A free standing building of this smaller size is unique to the market, and combined with the county island location and highest and best use challenges, comparables were difficult to obtain, even through discussions with appraisers. To account for this, a slight downward adjustment was made to the asking price from what the analysis might suggest.

A survey was conducted of buildings for sale and that had sold within a 5-mile radius of the property. A combination of office, retail, and mixed-use property was included in the survey. Special effort was made to seek out vacant buildings of similar size, potential use, and of similar lot size. To account for the uniqueness and challenges of the building, a slight downward adjustment to the asking price was made from what the analysis might suggest.

Lease Analysis

In order to establish a lease rate range for the building for use in the APOD, a lease survey was conducted of both existing office space and retail space within a 3-mile radius of the property. Although zoning for the property could allow both uses, most retail applications would require a special use permit from the County which may or may not be granted depending on the business type, so ultimately only the office lease comparables were used.

The property is unique to the market. Never the less, special effort was made to seek out free standing buildings available for lease and of comparable space sizes for lease.

APOD

The APOD was initially prepared as part of the pricing analysis and recommendations to the owner. It ultimately was used as part of the presentation package to prospective investor-buyers.

The lease rate of $16/sf modified gross was initially obtained through the lease survey and later supported during the marketing period by the unsolicited offers to lease in that rate range that I received. The CAP rates of 7.5% - 8% were intentionally kept above market to account for the newness of the pro forma tenant and to account for the additional perceived risk of a single tenant property.

Ground Lease Analysis

The ground lease analysis was prepared as an alternative marketing recommendation, but was discarded very early on due to the perceived complexity by the owner of this approach. Also, ground leasing for this type of property is unusual in this market, as is ground leasing in and of itself in this specific sub-market.

Two comparables were obtained from recent land sales of parcels literally right across the street from the subject property. A 31,300 square foot lot at a signalized intersection sold for $23.95/square foot in middle of year one, and an 11,500 square foot lot sold for $22.50/square foot two years earlier. A $24 price per square foot for the subject property was set, to account for appreciation from the comparable sales dates.

Based on $24/sf the subject 9,975 sf lot was valued at $239,400. Using a yield rate of 6.5%, which was slightly higher than long-term interest rates at the time but lower than the projected CAP for the property, the ground lease should generate income of about $15,500 per year or about $1.55/sf.

Subtracting the $239,400 lot value from the total asking price of $650,000 gives the building and improvements an asking price of $410,600 or about $112/sf. This building-only price would be supported during the marketing period from the offers received from owner-users looking for office/warehouse space.

After doing this analysis I became aware that a 700-acre office park under development on a nearby site (a few miles to the north and east of this property) was on a ground lease of $1.50 per square foot per year.

(As previously mentioned, the ground lease analysis very early on became an exercise only but will definitely be used in future presentations.)

Sales Comparison Analysis

The sales comparison analysis compiles data of the properties for sale and the ones that have most recently sold that are most similar to, and physically closest to, our subject property:

SALES COMPARISON

Address	Type	Size	Year Built	Price/SF
1212 Universe Lane	Office	5680	2005	$215
1111 W. Universe Lane	Retail	2078	2005	$235
1620 N. 82nd Avenue	Office	3080	1966	$149
* 8111 E. Thoms Road	Office	5455	2004	$170
* 3014 N. Hayman	Office	15,536	1974	$193
3666 N. Millstone Drive	Office	2511	1976	$198
7320 E. 6th Avenue	Office	1366	1969	$435
3610 N. 44th Street	Office	7091	1985	$178
* 1730 E. Bonita Blvd.	Retail	6800	Unknown	$81
2323 E. Universe Lane	Office	8985	Unknown	$150
3337 N. Millstone Drive	Office	4019	1982	$200

* Indicates sold/in escrow

Lease Comparison Analysis

As with the sales comparison analysis, the lease analysis compiles data of the properties for lease and the ones that have most recently been leased that are most similar to, and physically closest to, our subject property.

When conducting a lease analysis extreme caution must be taken to not mistake the asking lease rates from the rates that space is actually leased at. For example, the asking price for a certain space may be $15/square foot NNN but in reality, depending on many factors including the quality of the prospective tenant, the motivation of the landlord and the customized terms and conditions of a specific lease, the actual price that the space is leased at could be $12/square foot gross.

Remember, while somewhat misleading because no two leases are ever the same, 'NNN' refers to a triple-net lease where the tenants pays for all of the expenses associated with a given property, including building insurance, capital repairs and property taxes. Two other types of commonly used lease phrases are 'modified gross' and 'gross or full service' leases.

In both of these lease types the expenses of a property are split between the owner and the tenant. Ultimately, the owner of income property is concerned with the bottom line, or the income received, while the tenant is concerned with what its monthly rent check will be.

LEASE ANALYSIS

Address	Space Size	Rate	Type
1805 N. Scottsland Road	1044 - 1392	$9 - $14	Modified gross
2240 N. Scottsland Road	1500 - 3000	$14.75 - $18.50	Full service
1208 E. Broadway Road	866 - 2668	$16.50	Full service
1525 N. Granite Road	1307 - 2843	$12 - $14	NNN
2121 S. Millstone Drive	633 - 3500	$16	Full service
2226 S. Rowling Road	2780	$17	Modified gross
7340 E. Bonita Drive	9189	$25	NNN
1333 W. Broadstone Drive	6444	$18.25	Full service
398 S. Millstone Drive	585 - 1041	$24 - $26.67	Full service
1835 E. Universe Lane	900 - 1050	$14.86 - $16	Modified gross
2120 S. McFlint Avenue	1842	$14	Full service
1438 W. Broadway Road	2340	$16.50	Full service

Regional Analysis

The property is situated in the North Tempdale – South Scottsland Neighborhoods of the County Region. Tempdale and Scottsland are the 3rd and 4th largest cities in the County.

The County has a current population of 3,600,000 and since the beginning of the decade has grown by 14%. Over the next 30 years, assuming that growth trends remain relatively unchanged, the population is expected to grow to 6,300,000.

Job growth has averaged 5% annually since the beginning of the decade with the highest levels of growth in medium-wage jobs paying over $28,000 per year and high-wage jobs paying over $43,000 per year. The majority of high-wage jobs are concentrated in advanced business services, high-tech and software. Median household income is just over $46,000.

The cost of living is 99% of the US index, and regional unemployment as of the current year is 4.2% compared to a national average of 5%. 60% of the workforce has some college education or an associates degree or higher.

The City was recently rated the 12th best place to start a business by a well known and highly respected business magazine the beginning of the year. Area businesses have seen decreases in the average employer tax rate, along with individual income tax rates, over the past two years. The flat corporate income tax rate is just under 7% with individual income tax rates averaging 3.27%. Transaction privilege taxes in the Neighborhoods are between 8% - 8.2%. A variety of redevelopment tax credits are available.

The regional office vacancy rate as of the beginning of the year is 13.1% compared to 16.2% one year ago.

Neighborhood Analysis

Although the subject property is in the City of Tempdale, it is also about ½ mile from the City of Scottsland. Both Neighborhoods – North Tempdale and South Scottsland – are undergoing extensive redevelopment that is expected to have a positive affect on the property.

The property is sited on Scottsland Road, a major north-south route between North Tempdale and South Scottsland, with traffic counts of over 100,000 vehicles per day. The property is ¼ mile from the freeway on-off ramp. The freeway provides access from the southeast valley cities of Mensa, Gilding, Chandong and Tempdale to the northeast, central, and west valley cities of Scottsland, Photon, and Glencove. Mass transportation or foot traffic does not play a major role as of yet, but this is expected to change as densities increase and the infrastructure for this continues to develop.

South Scottsland Neighborhood

Scottsland is the 4th largest city in the Region. Since the beginning of the decade the population growth rates have slowed to a rate of just of 1.6% in the past year. The average unemployment rate was 3.9% last year, lower than the region's average, and for the past eight years has consistently run lower than the regional unemployment rate.

The South Scottsland Neighborhood is the established, mature part of Scottsland with much of the City's retail, entertainment and office activities located in this area. The population is nearly 101,000 with a median age of 40.5 and over 65% of the households have a median income of over $35K.

Scottsland's employment base is diversified with business services, high tech, biomedical, retail and tourism and mirrors the mixture of the North Tempdale Neighborhood.

Total office vacancy rates for the South Scottsland sub-market was 20% in the previous year but is expected to decline to 15% by the end of the current year.

Within a 5-mile radius of the subject property, the South Scottsland Neighborhood has a variety of investment activity planned or underway that should positively affect the subject property. These projects include:

1. University - Scottsland Innovation Center, a 1.2 million square foot research-office and retail development.
2. House Warehouse under new construction with additional 10,000 square feet of neighborhood retail.
3. A 37,500 square foot senior center & citizen service center next to 223 apartments under development.
4. A 41,000 square foot National Fitness Center recently built.
5. Plus another $55,000,000 of development and redevelopment activity planned or underway.

North Tempdale Neighborhood

Tempdale is the 4th largest city in the Region and is home to State University with over 84,000 students. Tempdale's population of 159,000 is expected to grow by 10% over the next five years. The average unemployment rate was 3.4% in the last year, lower than the region's average rate.

Tempdale offers the most educated work force in the area with over 40% of the residents 25 or older holding a Bachelor's degree or higher. Tempdale has urban environment amenities such as the University, Tempdale Town Lake (a 2-mile lake that receives more than 2 million visitors annually), loft living and a vibrant downtown. The population's a median age is 28.8 with an average household income of nearly $61,000.

Tempdale's employment base mirrors Scottsland's, with high levels of employment in business services, high tech and biomedical.

The office vacancy rate in the Downtown/North Tempdale area was 12.2% in the last year and is expected to remain about the same through the current year.

Within a 5-mile radius of the subject property, the North Tempdale Neighborhood has a variety of investment activity planned or underway that should positively affect the subject property. These projects include:

1. Tempdale Marketplace – a $200 million, 1.3 million square foot power/lifestyle/entertainment center located less than one mile from the subject property.

2. Tempdale Town Lakes projects – A variety of condominium, office, retail and hotel projects including Rio Best, Playa del Suerte, Rio Norte Santiago, Edgelake Condominiums and Tempdale Town Lake Apartments.

3. Richardson Docks Lakeside – A project consisting of over 790,000 square feet of office and retail space and over 400 lakefront condominiums.

4. Scottsland & Curry Road strip center – Directly across the street from the subject parcel is a 6,000 square foot neighborhood strip center under construction with rents running $25/sf NNN.

[While somewhat misleading because no two leases are ever the same, 'NNN' refers to a triple-net lease where the tenants pays for all of the expenses associated with a given property, including building insurance, capital repairs and property taxes. Two other types of commonly used lease phrases are 'modified gross' and 'gross or full service' leases. In both of these lease types the expenses of a property are split between the owner and the tenant. Ultimately, the owner of income property is concerned with the bottom line, or the income received, while the tenant is concerned with what its monthly rent check will be.]

Linkage Analysis

The population characteristics around the property should suggest that there are the Customer and Employee bases to support an office use and help to identify the type of office uses most likely supported.

Linkages

1. Proximity to Customers

We don't know specifically who the customers will be, but we can look at the population characteristics to determine if a general office use would be supported.

2. Proximity to Employees

We don't know specifically who the employees will be, but we can look at the population characteristics, specifically the education levels, age groups and existing travel times to work.

3. Neighboring Uses/Competing Uses

The property is in a growing, redeveloping area that is transitioning from a mixed-use industrial area in a county island to a more professional mixed-use office/retail area. Because of this activity, competing uses such as more office or retail space is anticipated and encouraged since it will have a positive affect on the redevelopment of the area.

Demographic Analysis

Free and premium resources along with information obtained from the City of Tempdale, City of Scottsland, and the County was used for this analysis.

The following reports were used in the order presented below.

The first step was to determine the likely service area radius in miles or drive times. Once the radius was identified the specific population characteristics could be analyzed.

A. Census Employment Report

1. 75% of the employed travel less than 29 minutes to work. This equates to a 5-mile radius around the property. Within that radius,
2. 60% are employed in occupations that suggest an office use – Clerical, executive, professional and sales.

This data identifies the service area of the property and the likely professional office uses for the property.

B. Business Summary Report

3. 55% are employed in white-collar occupations.
4. 75% of the establishments employ nine or fewer people. This is also the employee occupancy range that the building could accommodate.

C. Office Report

5. The population and employment levels are expected to grow, and the growth in office employment can be extrapolated from this.

D. Demographic Trend Report

      6. The 35-64 age groups are expected to increase by 6% - 18% over the next five years.
      7. The $50,000 - $150,000 household income categories are expected to increase by 7% - 55%.
      8. The average and median household incomes are expected to continue to increase.

The data from the above Reports demonstrates continued population growth in 'employable' and 'entrepreneurial' age groups.

E. Population Summary Report

      9. The holders of associates, bachelors and graduate degrees should continue to increase, which demonstrates the existence and growth of an educated workforce.

F. Income Summary Report

      10. This report shows a continued increase in disposable household incomes above $40,000. This increase in disposable income mirrors the demographic, age, and household income growth patterns previously noted.

Comparable Activities

The following three properties were selected as being the most similar to the subject property and were used to rationalize the assumptions and strategies developed for our subject property:

1. 1620 N. 82nd Street, Scottsland – This is a vacant 3,080 square foot free standing office building built in 40 years ago. The property has not been updated and is priced 'as is' at $460,000 or $149.35/square foot. It is located approximately two miles from the subject property and, except for the lack of updating, is most similar to the subject. The unit of comparison is price per square foot.

2. 3014 N. Hay Road, Scottsland – This is a multi-tenant 15,536 square foot office building with a 90% occupancy rate. The property is being sold as a net leased investment opportunity and is priced at $3,000,000 or $193.10/square foot and offers the investor a CAP rate of 7%. It is located approximately three miles from the subject property. The unit of comparison is the CAP rate as it relates to development of the pro forma APOD for the subject property.

3. 1111 W. University Drive, Tempdale – This is part of a new 8,000 square foot mixed-use office/retail condominium project. The property is 2,040 square feet and is priced at $489,000 or $235.32/square foot. It is located approximately four miles from the subject property. The unit of comparison is price per square foot and the use-type of the space.

Annual Property Operating Data Report

The Annual Property Operating Data Report is used to calculate your actual cash flow. Much of the data entry on the annual property operating data report is self explanatory.

Here are a several items of note to consider:

1. At the top right corner of the form you'll want to enter not only your purchase or acquisition price for the property, but also all associated expenses such as buyer broker fees, closing costs, inspection fees, and legal and accounting fees to review the purchase contract.

2. The bulk of the Report has to do with your current actual and your projected income and expenses. These can be calculated on a monthly or annual basis - just be sure to keep your amounts consistent. For example, if you're using a monthly projection don't forget to divide your building insurance fees by 12 to arrive at a monthly figure, since these are usually paid annually.

3. Line #1 of the Report is your projected rental income at a 100% occupancy rate. To arrive at this number you will use your current actual rents plus your projected rents if there are any vacant spaces to be leased. It is always a good idea to use several rent scenarios, with rents increasing and with rents decreasing, to allow for any fluctuations in the market. A common mistake that inexperienced investors make is to assume that rents will always continue to rise.

4. Line #2 is where you make a reduction in your gross rental income due to vacancies or collections (eviction) losses. As with your rental income projections, it is always a good idea

to use various vacancy rates. In particular, if your property is purchased using financing, be sure to calculate your 'zero' line, the point where your net operating income, less your operating expenses, less all other expenses including your mortgage payment, equals 'zero'. This of course means you are making no profit on the property but you are covering all of your expenses. Obviously, this is also the point that you do not want to go past, i.e. you do not want to have negative cash flow.

5. On lines #11, #12 and #13 are employee costs associated directly with the property. For example, a large shopping complex or apartment building may have on-site management or leasing dedicated specifically to that property.

6. Line #23, Miscellaneous Services, would include expenses such as landscaping, fire alarm inspections, and pool service for apartment properties.

7. Line #32, Participation Payments, refers to a group investing structure. If the property was purchased by several people or partners, part of the purchase agreement may call for income to be distributed on a regular basis to the owners.

8. Line #33, Leasing Commissions, refers to any brokerage fees you pay in conjunction with the leasing of vacant suites. Customarily, leasing fees are paid in advance in one lump sum while the income from the lease is realized by the owner over a period of time.

9. Line #34, Funded Reserves, refers to money that is being set aside for future capital improvements. In the beginning of this book we discussed how when buying investment real estate you are almost always buying somebody else's problem. The key to success is to accurately identify those problems and understand the costs associated with solving them. For example, you may have determined that the property will need a new roof or need to have the parking lot repaved five years from now. Rather than going out of pocket

at the time the repair is needed, you will want to have the property generate enough cash flow to be able to set aside income monthly in your capital reserve fund.

Annual Property Operating Data Report

Subject Property _____

Address _____
Property Type _____
Size of Property _____ (Sq. Ft./Units)

Purpose of Report _____

Acquisition Price _____
Plus Acquisition Costs _____
Plus Loan Fees/Costs _____
Less Mortgages _____
Equals Initial Investment _____

Assessed/Appraised Values
Land   0 _____
Building   0 _____
Personal Property 0   0%
Total   0   100%

	Balance	Periodic Pmt	Pmts/Yr	Interest	Amort Period	Loan Term
1st			12			
2nd			12			

Adjusted Basis as of: _____

Annual or Monthly	$/SQ FT or $/Unit	% of GOI	Expense	Income	Notes
1 POSSIBLE RENTAL INCOME					
2 Less: Vacancy & Losses					
3 ADJUSTED RENTAL INCOME					
4 Plus: Other Income					
5 GROSS OPERATING INCOME (GOI)					
OPERATING EXPENSES					
7 Property Taxes					
8 Personal Taxes					
9 Property Insurance					
10 Management Fees					
11 Payroll - Property					
12 Expenses/Benefits - Property					
13 Employee Taxes - Property					
14 Repairs and Maintenance					
Utilities:					
15					
16					
17					
18					
19 Accounting, Legal, Prof Fees					
20 Licenses/Permits					
21 Advertising and Marketing					
22 Supplies					
23 Miscellaneous Services					
24					
25					
26					
27					
28					
29 TOTAL OPERATING EXP					
30 NET OPERATING INCOME					
31 Less: Mortgage Payment					
32 Less: Participation Payments					
33 Less: Leasing Commissions					
34 Less: Funded Reserves					
35 CASH FLOW BEFORE TAXES					

Author: _____

Read More

If you found this book useful please consider leaving a review at your point of purchase!

Remember, it's a well kept secret in buying investment real estate that you are almost always buying the seller's problem. However, that doesn't mean you shouldn't buy your chose property, it simply means that you should be able to accurately identify any problems and the costs associated with solving those problems, before you sign the contract to purchase.

For example, let's say the current use for a building is a multi-tenant office property with a high vacancy rate and you (as the buyer) want to turn it into offices for your business. Or an apartment building needs significant capital improvements, such as a roof repair or replacement of a majority of the HVAC units. Or a retail property sits very close to a school or to a church, a situation that current zoning laws may prohibit your leasing to certain types of tenants, thereby reducing the number of potential business types you can market your vacant retail suites to.

The key is to accurately identify the existing and potential problems, and the likely costs associated with solving those problems. In *The Real Estate Property Management Guide* I discuss all aspects of property management, including the steps to take when considering what type of investment property is right for you. After all, just because you can buy or finance an acquisition doesn't mean that you should actually invest in it.

In this book, *Investment Real Estate Analysis: A Case Study*, we have drilled-down on the specific analysis used by all professional investment real estate brokers and buyers to determine the strengths and weaknesses - and to identify the hidden opportunities - when deciding how to position a piece of real estate for sale. While this case study was written from the seller perspective, as a potential buyer you should *always* apply these same steps yourself to gain a thorough understanding of what you are buying - before you sign the purchase contract!

For more information on real estate investing and property management please visit my website at http://HowToPropertyManage.com

Here's to your real estate investing success!

Jeffrey Roark

About The Author

Investment Real Estate Analysis is written under the pen name Jeffrey Roark.

A pen name is used because the "real Jeff" currently owns and operates a private investment brokerage in the Western U.S. Since the intent of this book is not to gain business for his brokerage, or share market-specific trade secrets, he has chosen this anonymous form of authorship.

Rest assured, *Investment Real Estate Analysis* is based on over a quarter-century of actual, real-life experience. It is not academic, classroom or theoretical. Jeff's clients pay him a lot of money for information you're about to receive.

Jeff began his real estate career over 25 years ago in the Midwest by investing primarily in his own investment portfolio. Over the past 15 years he has personally brokered millions of dollars worth of real estate sales and lease transactions for his clients in retail, office, industrial, single-family and multi-family residential income properties, and in raw and subdivided land.

He is a Certified Commercial Investment Member. The CCIM designation is held by only 15,000 commercial and investment real estate professionals worldwide and is the highest professional certification one can earn in commercial investment real estate.

Jeff currently owns and operates a private investment brokerage located in the Western U.S. that provides sales, leasing and property management services to its clients. Those clients range from single-property investors to owners of large commercial portfolios. The firm's advice to its clients is straightforward and based on the realities of the marketplace.

Investment Real Estate Analysis provides the same candid advice.

For more information on real estate investing and property management please visit my website at http://HowToPropertyManage.com

www.ingramcontent.com/pod-product-compliance
Lightning Source LLC
Chambersburg PA
CBHW070837180526
45168CB00002B/860